MEL BAY PRESENTS

THE GUITAR SCALES

VOL·1
GUITAR TAB

BY PHILIPPE GANTER

CD CONTENTS

1	Tuning notes (open strings) [:53]		19	Improvisation exercise # 3 - Chord Progression 1 [3:36]
2	The famous Blues lick [:35]		20	Improvisation exercise # 3 - Chord Progression 2 [3:33]
3	Chapter 1 exercise [:39]		21	Dorian mode, format 5 (C) [:14]
4	Major Pentatonics : vertical motion (C) [2:00]		22	Dorian ascending format shifts (G) [1:55]
5	Improvisation exercise # 1 - Chord Progression 1 [3:46]		23	Dorian descending format shifts (G) [1:55]
6	Improvisation exercise # 1 - Chord Progression 2 [3:31]		24	Dominant ascending format shifts (C) [1:52]
7	Minor Pentatonics : vertical motion (A) [1:59]		25	Dominant descending format shifts (C) [1:53]
8	Improvisation exercise # 2 - Chord Progression 1 [3:34]		26	Improvisation exercise # 4 - Chord Progression 1 [3:26]
9	Improvisation exercise # 2 - Chord Progression 2 [3:36]		27	Improvisation exercise # 4 - Chord Progression 2 [3:36]
10	Major Scales : the 7 formats (F) [2:17]		28	Major Pentatonic, format 2 - Groups of 3 (E) [:24]
11	Chapter 4 warm-up exercise [2:08]		29	Dominant, format 2 - Groups of 3 (A) [:35]
12	Major Scales : vertical study (C) [3:32]		30	Major Pentatonic, format 5 - Groups of 4 (Bb) [:26]
13	Shapes with open strings (E, D, B, A, G, F) [3:04]		31	Dorian, format 7 - Groups of 4 (A) [:40]
14	Major Scale ascending format shifts (G) [1:29]		32	Major Pentatonic, format 3 - Thirds & fourths (Eb) [:23]
15	Major Scale ascending study (G) [1:51]		33	Major Scale, format 5 - Thirds (D) [:32]
16	Major Scale descending format shifts (G) [1:30]		34	Minor Pentatonic, format 1 - Fifths (B) [:21]
17	Major Scale descending study (G) [1:37]		35	Dominant, format 5 - Fourths (E) [:27]
18	Major Scale complete study (D) [3:09]			

I.D. MUSIC

© 1998 BY I.D. MUSIC
29 RUE DE BITCHE (PARIS-LA-DÉFENSE) 92400 COURBEVOIE - FRANCE
EXCLUSIVE SALES AGENT: MEL BAY PUBLICATIONS, INC., #4 INDUSTRIAL DRIVE, PACIFIC, MO 63069.

Visit us on the Web at www.melbay.com — E-mail us at email@melbay.com — Fax: 636-257-5062

Contents

Contents

Definition

The purpose of all musical instruments is to produce sound in various ways:

1 - Without any definite pitch (**percussions**);

2 - Simultaneously (**chords**);

3 - As a sequence (**melodies**).

Some instruments allow two of these options, some can combine all three.

Most melodic instruments can be used to select several notes out of the twelve existing in occidental music, in order to play a melody. It can be a theme (head of a song or a musical piece), a harmonic figure (*riff*, arpeggio, bass line) or an improvisation (*solo*).

Scales are sets of notes arranged in sequence, designed to be partly incorporated in these musical constructions. By definition, a scale is a **sequence of notes, ordered in a direction** (up or down), **within the range of one octave** (six whole tones).

"An order" and "in the same direction" mean that a scale can either be **ascending or descending**. By no means will it include, in its basic form, back and forth motion. C - D - F - E is not a scale in itself, as opposed to C - D - E - Bᵇ.

The ascending and descending notes are the same, apart from one exception called melodic minor scale, which is actually formed from two different scales. Melodic minor will be covered in *volume 2*.

"Within an octave" means that the sequence will be exactly the same - nothing removed, nothing added - for any octave, up or down. Therefore a scale has no relationship to the range where it is played.

For the sake of simplicity, we will call a scale any set of notes in sequence between any note and the one that is an octave higher.

1

Basics

Scales, use of

Practicing scales extends one's set of tools for improvisation and general playing, but also physical technique, and a stronger command of the notes on the instrument. Even (bad) teachers who merely ask for scale practicing eventually get results from their surviving pupils.

Although mandatory as part of musical study, technical practice including scales will amount to a useless and thankless task without a lot of application such as learning tunes, composing, arranging, performance, improvising, jamming and other real life, one-night-stand hot stuff.

As far as the guitar is concerned, learning scales is made even more exciting by the string instruments distinctive characteristic - a lot of different ways to play the same thing at different locations on the fingerboard - which involves two opposite features:

✿ Plus : notes that are far apart can be reached easier than, for instance on a keyboard. The guitarist can cover a wide range with just two or three fingers.

✿ Minus : he needs to learn several ways of playing the same musical item, otherwise he will have to face the inconvenience of knowing only one shape for each chord, scale or musical idea, his left hand furiously moving back and forth all the way up and down the fingerboard !

Formats

In this method, each shape a scale can visually take, depending on the position where it is played on the fingerboard we will call its "**format**". This principle lies on the **tonic** notion.

The **tonic** is the main note of the scale, to which it gives its alphabet name, like the root of a chord is the basic note that the chord is named after. The root of a C chord is the note C, similarly the tonic of a C scale will also be the note C. The different **steps** (each one of the scale notes) are numbered from the tonic, which is therefore step 1, on which the scale is built.

At any place on the fingerboard, the **format** of a scale - or any other musical item, for that matter - is identified by the locations where the **tonic** can be found without changing positions. The **position** is defined as the number of the fret on - or above - which the index finger is placed at a given time, in other words without moving the left hand (for right-handed guitarists).

The locations where the tonic appears on various strings (2 or 3 for a given position) make up a simple shape, around which the musical item is wrapped. It is quite easy to remember these few two or three note tonic **patterns,** which are the basis of most fingerboard objectives such as scales, but also chords or melodies.

This idea of **patterns** as guidelines for playing scales, based upon the simple tonic shapes, was introduced in the 70's by the great *Howard Roberts* and has helped thousands of guitar students memorize, learn and use their musical tools.

Tonic **patterns,** and the **formats** that are built around them, are simple geometrical **markers** that will help you understand, memorize and play musical items at various places on the guitar fingerboard, offering you the widest field for their use and application.

Any musical item can roughly be played on as many places ("positions") as the number of different notes it is made of. Each one of these places will ask for a different fingering to play the same notes: these fingerings are the different **formats** to this item.

For each one of these positions, its **tonic** will appear two or three times at different octaves, thus forming a pattern around which the fingering can be drawn.

This **pattern** is the basis of the corresponding **format.**

Let's take as an example the following famous blues lick:

This sequence can be played over a **D** or **D7** chord, the tonic of which is the note D. This lick is built on four main notes (D, F#, A, C, in other words the **D7** arpeggio) and can be played in least four different spots:

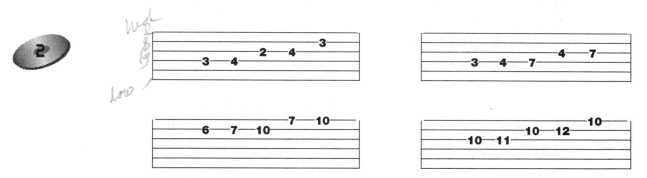

The **tonic** D is in various places depending on the position, whether the note D itself is included in the musical item or not:

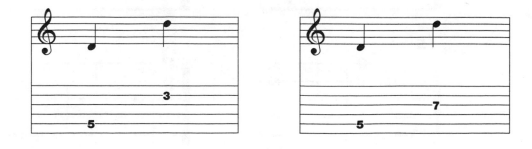

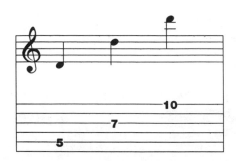 

These four figures make simple, easy to remember visual patterns:

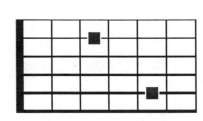 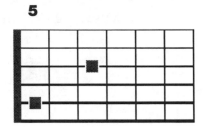

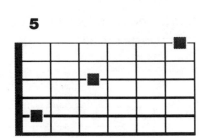 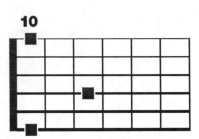

We then add the actual notes around each one of the patterns in order to create the four **formats** we have played for this lick:

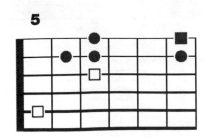 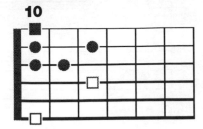

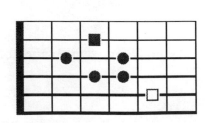 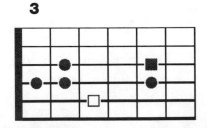

Practice guidelines

This pattern/format notion is most important in guitar scales study, for there are many ways to play any sequence of notes on the fingerboard.

We have chosen in this book to select one format, therefore one tonic pattern for each step of the scale. For example, a five notes scale will be learned and practiced through five formats supported by five patterns, at five locations on the fingerboard.

This brings about our **#1 guideline** : to be able to play any scale you learn and practice **from any step on any string**.

We also stress, for all scales, the use of fingerings that allow a balanced right hand motion, with notes as evenly dispatched on the strings as possible - the ideal being the same number of notes on all strings. This approach helps to build a smooth melodic execution.

Therefore, our **#2 guideline** is : to be able to play any scale in a way that requires an **equal or close number of notes** on each string.

First exercise

 This will help warm up your fingers before actual scales practicing and should be done on a daily basis :

The above sequence is based on finger combination **1 2 3 4 - 4 3 2 1**.

Feel free to try out the following and connect them without interruption:

✿ 2 1 3 4 - 4 3 1 2

✿ 3 1 2 4 - 4 2 1 3

✿ 4 1 2 3 - 3 2 1 4

Also, from now on keep in mind back and forth right hand motion:

✿ if you play with a pick, one stroke down, the next stroke up;

✿ if you use your fingers, one finger after the other (thumb/index ou index/middle finger).

2

Major
Pentatonic
Scales

Structure

Easy fingerings, logical visual shapes and a reduced set of notes to learn and play, make the use of **pentatonics** the simplest thing to do on the guitar.

Major pentatonic scales are made of five steps (numbered in roman letters below) two or three half tones apart from each other (a half tone is one fret up or down on the same string).

Taking the note C as the tonic, we now can build the **C major pentatonic scale**:

We can see that it is indeed a **C** (the tonic) **major** (including this tonic's major third, E) **pentatonic** (five notes) **scale** (sequence of notes, following an order, in the same direction).

Pentatonic scales are used in a lot of improvised music as well as several traditional music styles such as celtic, european, asian, etc.

It is # 1 for rock n'roll, country music or many jazz forms, and probably remains the most popular scale in the world.

Formats

There are **five** plug and play fingerings for this scale, working on the previous chapter's principles of one step, one format and as many notes on every string (two in this case). **Tonic** locations are figured on each diagram by **square** dots.

From the **tonic**:

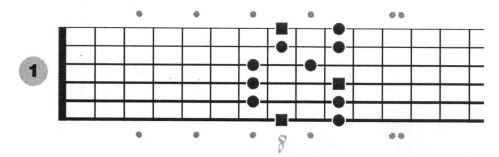

From the **second** step, D:

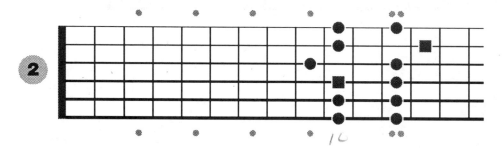

From the **third** step, E:

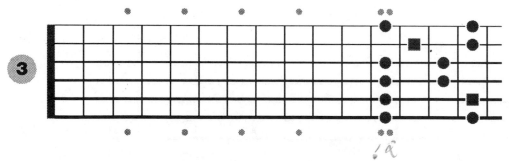

Same diagram but with **open strings** (circles on the left of the fingerboard):

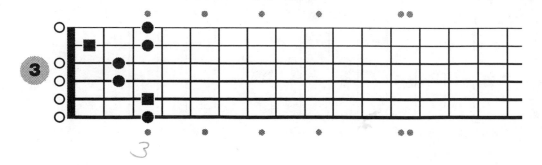

From the **fourth** step, G:

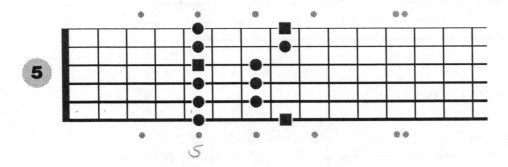

From the **fifth** step, A:

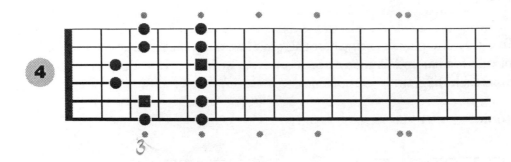

Patterns

By isolating the **tonics** in each diagram, we get the drawing for the five **patterns** that support these **pentatonic** scales:

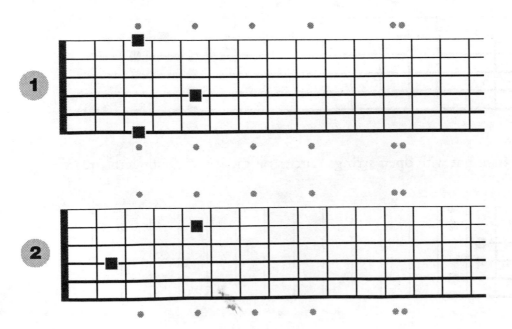

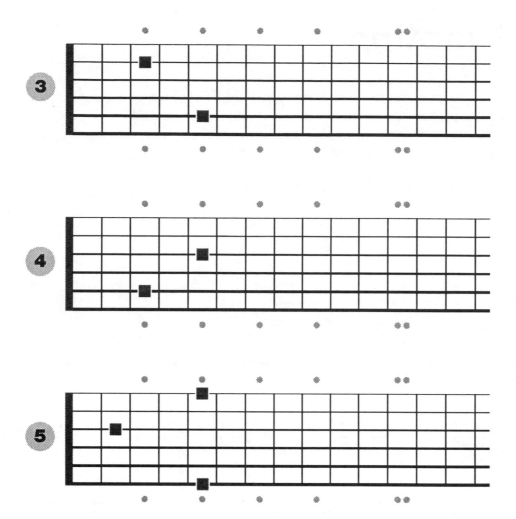

Let's take this opportunity to make some additional remarks about formats and patterns. The following principles apply to all scales:

✿ Formats are **numbered** from the **lowest note** in their fingerings: the step number is the format number. The number will be the same for the pattern we get for each format by removing all notes but the tonics just like we did above.

✿ Knowing the **pattern** is the **first** step when memorizing a scale. Notes that wrap around that tonic pattern to make up the format are to be learned afterwards. If you just can play the scale's tonics (the pattern) you've got yourself started. Conversely, if you can play a fingering without knowing the note that gives its name to the scale, sadly it may very well be useless!

✿ In order to **transpose** a scale, formats and patterns will come in handy: shift your pattern on the fingerboard up or down (e.g. to play Ds instead of Cs) then apply the format's fingering to that new position… and there you have it! Of course, this is true for any musical item on the guitar, not only for scales.

Vertical motion

Practicing the scales from the bottom E string should be avoided as a general rule, the goal being to be able to play any scale from any place on the fingerboard. We'll begin with a motion starting from the tonic (C in the example) then move up the strings, down and up again, back to the same note.

Left hand fingerings follow a universal system:

- ✿ 0: open string
- ✿ 1: index finger
- ✿ 2: middle finger
- ✿ 3: third finger
- ✿ 4: little finger

Let's start with the easiest format, #5 which is also, with a C tonic, located right in the middle of the fingerboard:

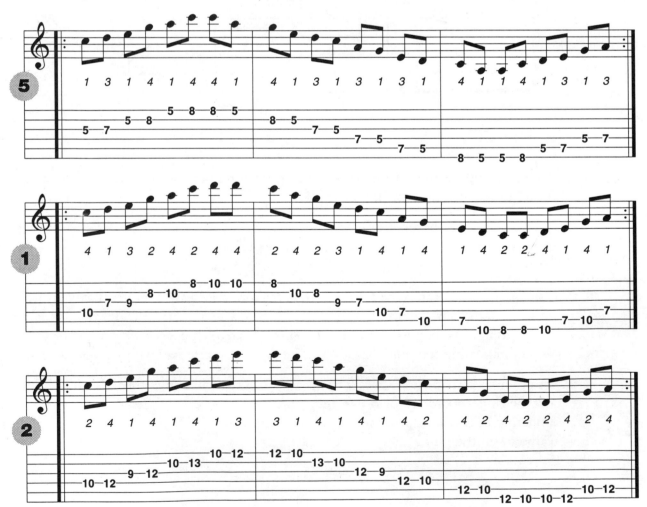

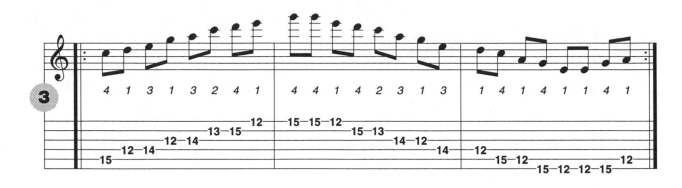

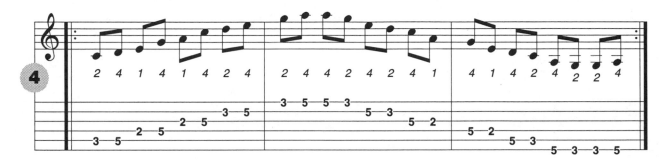

The first format presented (here #5) is not necessarily the first one to start with all of the time. On the contrary, you'd want to begin in various places to gradually get a clear grasp of the whole fingerboard.

On the other hand, the **order** 1, 2, 3, 4, 5, 1 etc. should be followed strictly no matter which format you choose to start with, so you can get ready to practice shifting formats later on.

The above exercise must be **transposed** and practiced for each **key**. Hold each note as long as possible and **don't go too fast**.

It is worthless trying to practice any scale without the use of a **metronome**.

Improvisation exercise #1

Once you have mastered your five formats for all 12 possible tonics, the next thing is to learn how to use them and incorporate them in your playing. Here is our first improvisation exercise : **major pentatonic** over a **major key.**

1 - Write down your own chord progression in the same key (one different key each day).

2 - Learn it.

3 - Record it (if you're by yourself) or have a fellow guitarist or pianist play it for you.

4 - Find on the fingerboard the appropriate major pentatonic scale, following the five formats.

5 - Practice shifting from one format to the other so as not to get "stuck" in one place on the fingerboard but to be able to move in either direction wherever you want to…

6 - Practice each format with a metronome, playing steady eight notes (two notes per beat).

7 - Same thing over the chord changes you've recorded, or while your kind fellow plays them for you.

8 - Improvise over the chord changes, using only the scale you've practiced.

9 - Improvise freely over the chord changes.

Pre-recorded changes

Two chord progressions are recorded on the CD for you to begin your improvisation exercise #1. The first one is in C major, the other in E major. You can use these tracks for the steps above, before you start writing your own!

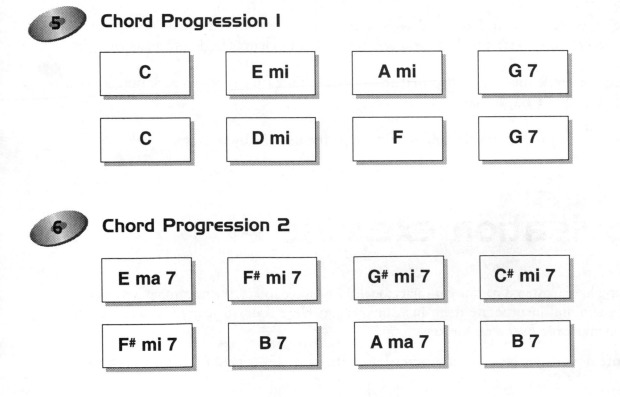

Chord Progression 1

C	E mi	A mi	G 7
C	D mi	F	G 7

Chord Progression 2

E ma 7	F# mi 7	G# mi 7	C# mi 7
F# mi 7	B 7	A ma 7	B 7

3

Minor Pentatonic Scales

Structure

The **minor pentatonic scale** is based upon the same structure but starting from the fifth (last) step. Step **V** thus becomes **I**, step **I** becomes **II** and so on.

The resulting scale is obviously also made of five steps:

If we start from our old **C major pentatonic** scale, with its tonic C...

... and we **shift** the steps so as to begin with the tonic **A** as the new tonic...

... we simply get an **A minor pentatonic** scale.

Therefore, it can be stressed that the notes are the same for **C major pentatonic** and **A minor pentatonic**. As far as pentatonics are concerned, the first "major" step is the second "minor" step.

This leads up to the **relative scales** notion, defined as one major scale and one minor scale made of the exact same notes out of which the tonic is different. The only difference is the note referred to as the tonic!

Formats

 The five minor pentatonic scale formats are thus, strictly the same as for the major ones.

Starting from our new tonic A, vertical motion fingerings become:

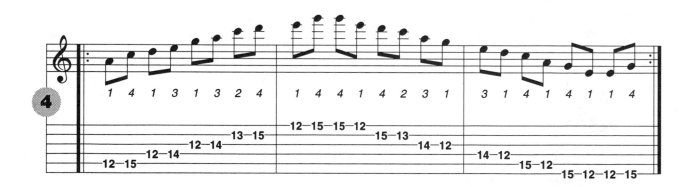

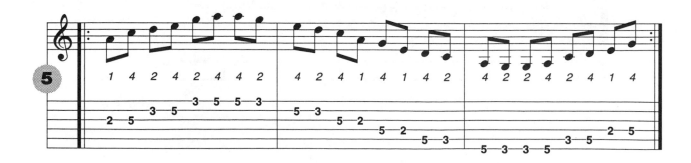

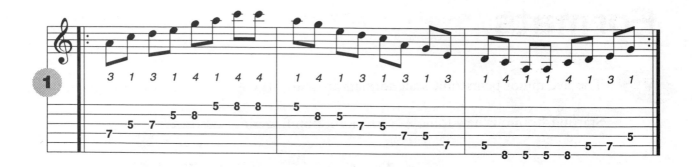

The five fingering formats and tonic patterns will be identical to the major ones, but their numbering will be different since the original major **Is** become the minor **IIs**...

Turning a major pentatonic to its relative minor pentatonic scale follows a simple arithmetic operation: the notes being the same for both of them, it is enough to change **tonics** and thus **formats**.

The fingering will be the same for both **C major pentatonic** format **2** and **A minor pentatonic** format **3**. The note thought of as the tonic for the first one is C (string 2, fret 13 and string 4, fret 10) and for the other one is A (string 2, fret 10 and string 5, fret 12).

It ensues from all these observations that a firm, final and all in all quite handy rule can be stated in this matter:

major format + 1 = minor format

For example, a major pentatonic format 4 looks and sounds exactly as a minor pentatonic format 5.

Applying this principle makes it easy to combine formats and tonic patterns.

Pentatonic format I...

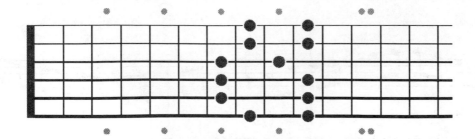

... traced over pentatonic pattern 2

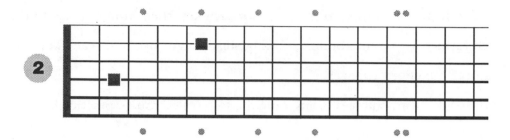

... produces our minor pentatonic format 2.

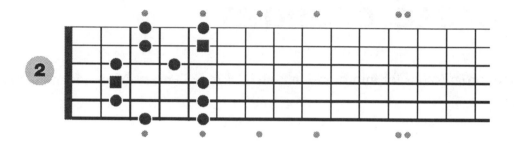

You can use this little trick or any other of your choice. Combining **patterns** and **formats** is an efficient, visual key to memorizing the many scales you'll have to learn, and will help you get more out of it with less effort...

Improvisation exercise #2

Minor pentatonic scales are obviously to be used over corresponding minor keys. Our second improvisation exercise will combine **major pentatonic** over a **major key** and **minor pentatonic** over a **minor key.**

1 - Write down your own chord progression in two keys, one major and one minor, four bars of each (one different set of keys each day). If you find it too difficult to connect major and minor pentatonic scales rightaway, you can insert an intermediate exercise between # 1 and #2, by practicing two major keys then two minor keys, and finally one of each. Please avoid the temptation of using two relative scales!

2 - Learn it.

3 - Record it (if you're by yourself) or have your fellow guitarist or pianist play it for you.

4 - Find on the fingerboard the appropriate major and minor pentatonic scales, following the five formats for both of them.

5 - Practice shifting from one format to the other for each key, then from one key to the next.

6 - Practice each format with a metronome, playing steady eight notes for each key.

7 - Same thing over the chord changes.

8 - Improvise over the chord changes, using only the two scales you've practiced.

9 - Improvise freely over the chord changes.

Pre-recorded changes

The two chord progressions for improvisation exercise #2 are D major/A minor and C minor/ G major.

8 **Chord Progression 1**

D	B mi	A 7	D
A mi	B mi 7 (b5)	E 7	A mi

9 **Chord Progression 2**

C mi 7	F mi 7	D mi 7 (b5)	G 7
E mi 7	A mi 7	D 7	G ma 7

4

Introducing Major Scales

Structure

We have now learned major and minor pentatonic scales which are based upon five note structures, as the name indicates.

There is a **seven** note scale (as its name does not indicate) called the **major scale**. Its actual name is "major diatonic scale", **diatonic** meaning that it is made up of notes:

1 - Acoustically linked to the tonic in ways we won't detail here but that are the basis of their use in composition and improvisation. It can be said that these notes have a common **harmonic affinity"** which is the reason why, for example, no C major scale note will really be wrong on a C major chord indeed even on any chord of the C major key.

2 - One half tone or one whole tone apart from each other, no more. The major pentatonic scale, for instance, is not diatonic since it comprises two minor thirds (between its steps **III** and **IV** and between **V** and **I**).

The most popular diatonic scales include seven notes and are often derived from our **major scale** which, in fact is nothing more than a **major pentatonic** scale (tonic, second, major third, fifth, sixth), to which the **fourth** and the **major seventh** are added.

The resulting scale structure is:

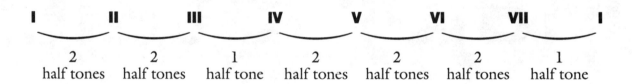

Taking C as the tonic:

Formats

Keeping in mind the first chapter's guidelines, we shall practice these scales with **three notes** on each **string** and one fingering **format** for each **step**. Let's take F major as an example and see what the seven formats are :

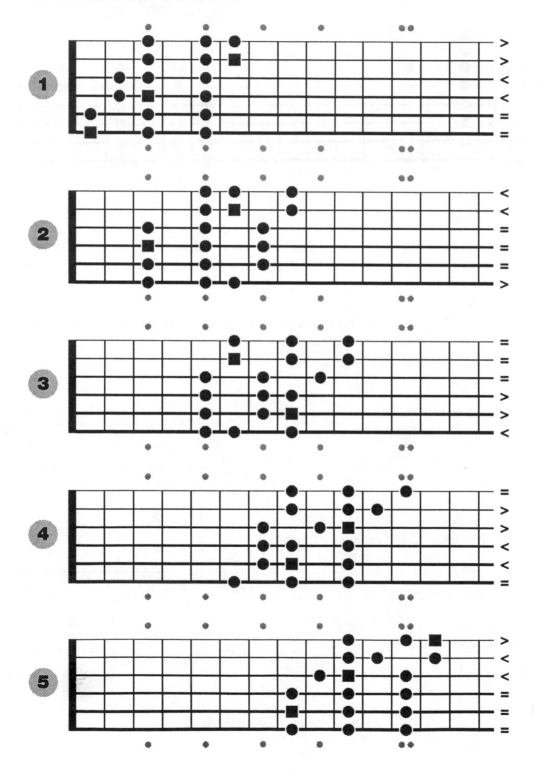

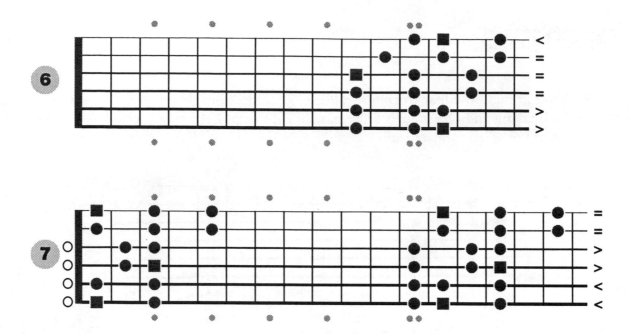

Symbols used for each string (<, = and >) can help you cut down on your effort when memorizing and practicing major as well as other diatonic scales that we will cover later on in this method.

You can see quite easily that all the fingerings above are built on three basic constructions, that we will call **fingering items** :

I - Whole tone + whole tone, that we can call the **normal item**, represented by the equal sign =.

This item is played with fingers 1, 2 and 4.

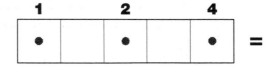

2 - Half tone + whole tone, that we can call the **open item**, represented by the inferior sign <.

This item is also played with fingers 1, 2 and 4.

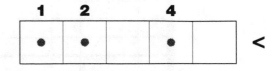

3 - Whole tone + half tone, that we can call the **closed item**, represented by the superior sign >.

This item is played with fingers 1, 3 and 4.

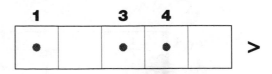

Fingerings

Here are the notes and fingerings we get from the above F major scale diagrams. To keep it clear and readable, we have chosen to use a $\frac{12}{8}$ time signature and write groups of three eight notes, which is the same as triplets in $\frac{4}{4}$, hence the CD count-up (four dotted quarter notes).

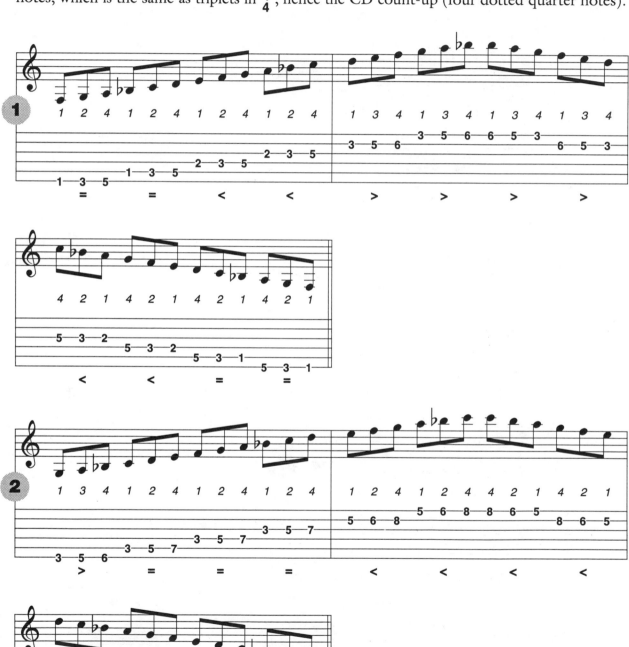

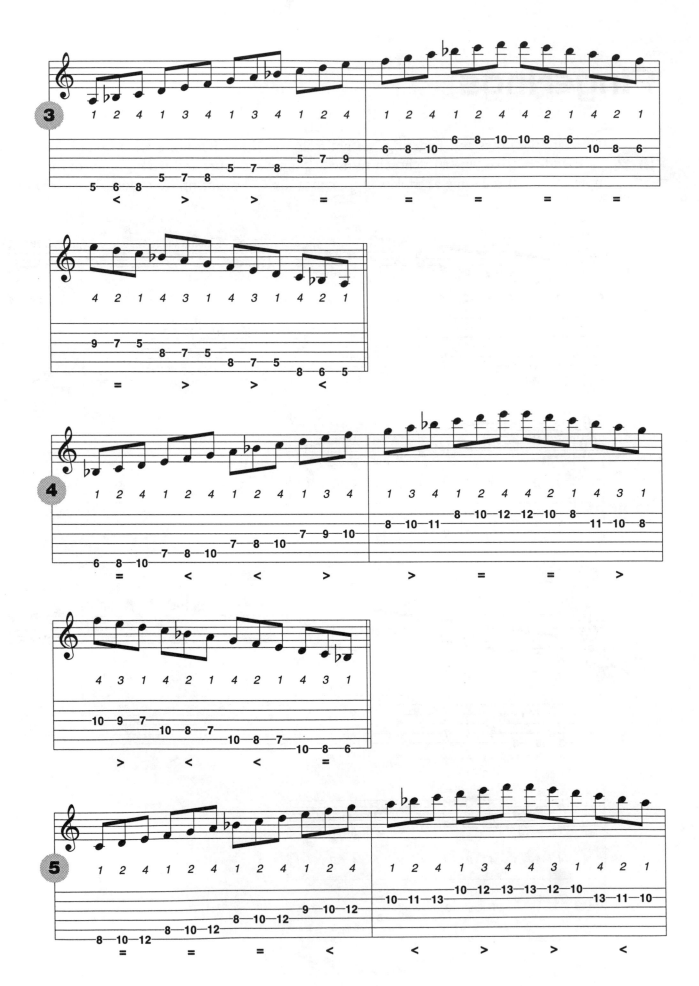

The interest in these formats compared to the pentatonic ones can be immediately seen : **diagonal** playing. Keep in mind it is essential to develop one's ability to move horizontally on the fingerboard rather than just vertically while practicing scales, or chords and sightreading.

Each one of these formats spreads out over six or seven frets thus allowing a richer, extended playing.

Patterns

The extraction of the tonics for each format produces our seven "diatonic" patterns :

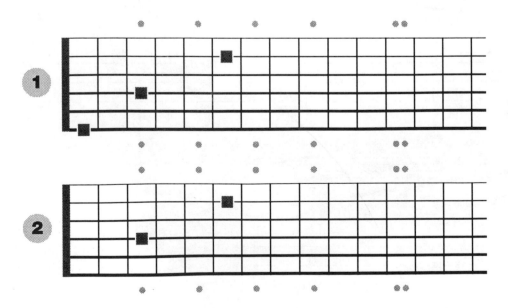

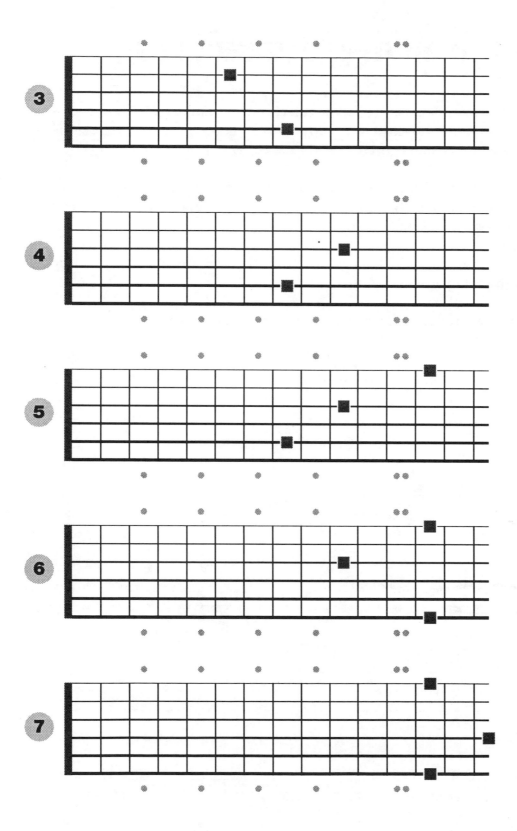

You should have these patterns down cold, since you will find many uses for them from now on! As with pentatonics - or any musical item - you will first find and learn the **patterns** for each format, before you proceed in adding the other notes to eventually end up with the whole fingering.

Another warm-up exercise

Here's another one, designed to follow the chapter 1 warm-up. It consists of playing each fingering item up and down on every string. The "normal" item, being the most difficult, is played twice. String numbers are circled (6 = low E string).

Practice with a metronome, **slowly** and **without breaking tempo.** Never go past the point where muscles hurt, the only result would be to damage your hands. Hold each note as long as possible before you play the next.

This exercise will help you build finger independence and strength if played daily, before you carry on with scale practicing by itself.

NB : From now on, left hand fingerings are only represented by <, = or >, except where fingering items as described on page 28 don't apply.

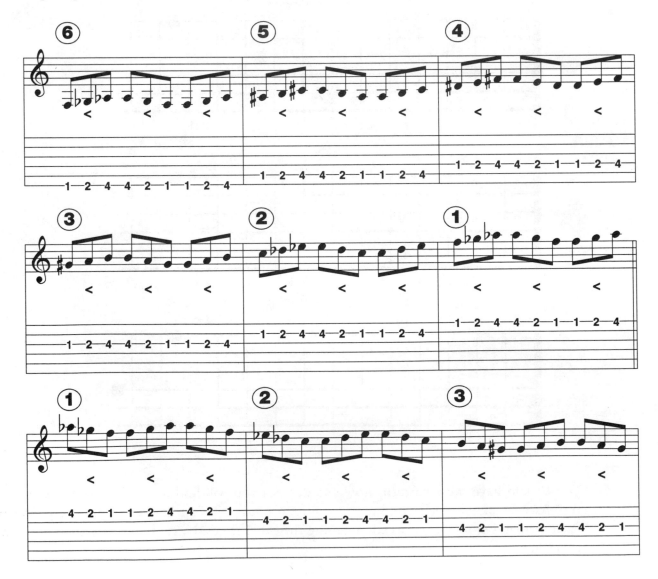

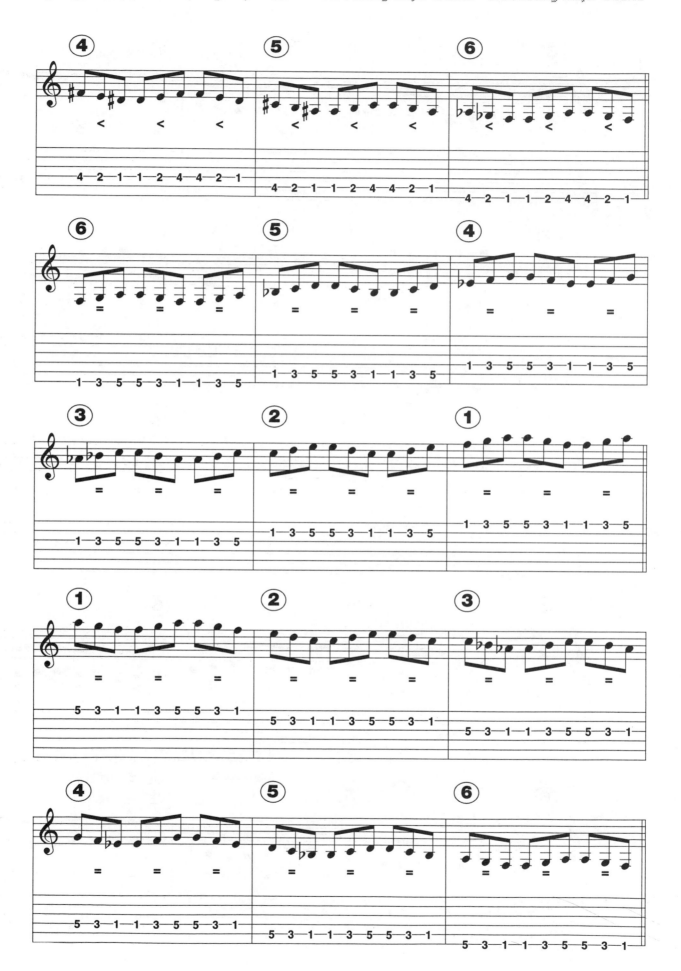

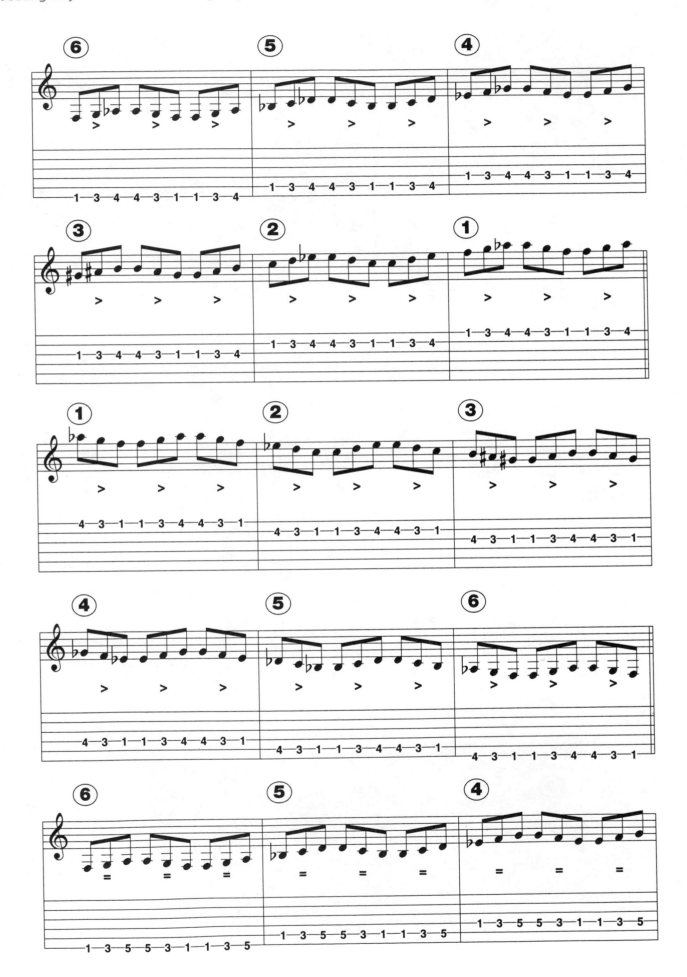

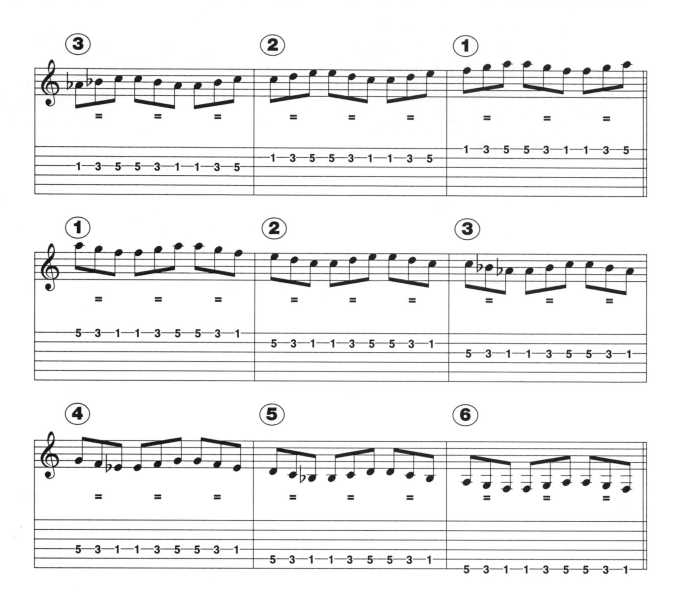

Progression chart

The chart on the following page can be used to keep track of your daily progress.

Write down each day the tempo as well as the number of times you repeated the exercise, allowing a short break between each repeat.

Tempos should always be slow enough to avoid making mistakes or break smoothness of execution. They can vary daily, plus or minus, like the number of times you repeat an exercise.

Start with comfortable values, like dotted quarter notes = 60 and only one time through. Do not hesitate to lower the tempo if needed.

Your goal could be around dotted quarter notes = 120 and four times through.

Date	Tempo	Times through
	60	1

Date	Tempo	Times through
	120	4

Major Scales Exercises

Vertical motion

You should be able to find out by yourself how to build the major diatonic scale exercises for all 7 formats in all 12 keys. Keep in mind the basics we listed in chapter 2 regarding pentatonics.

Here are some guidelines, in C major. Format sequence : 6, 7, 1, 2, 3, 4, 5. Once again, feel free to start anywhere and vary your practice in this way.

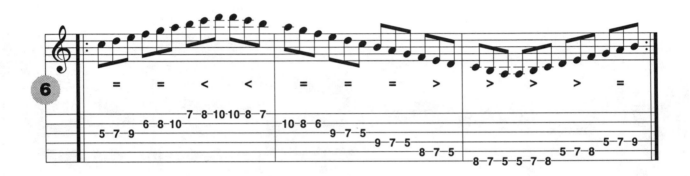

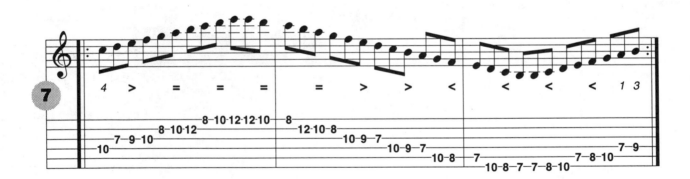

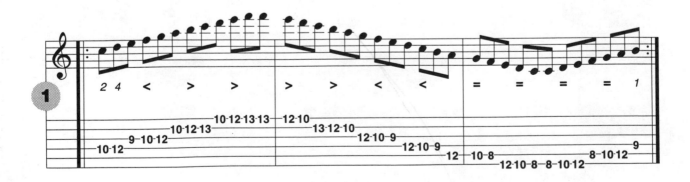

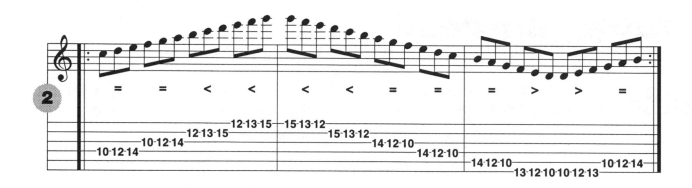

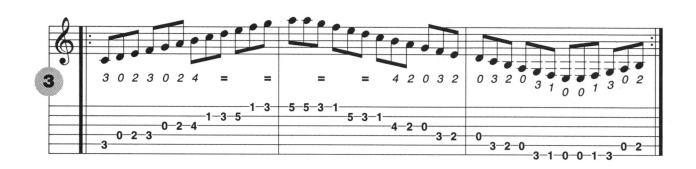

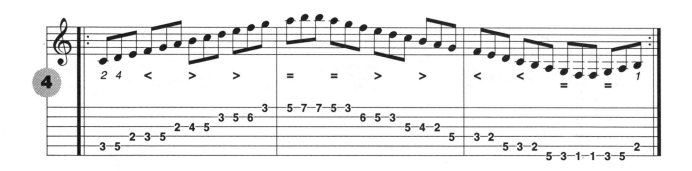

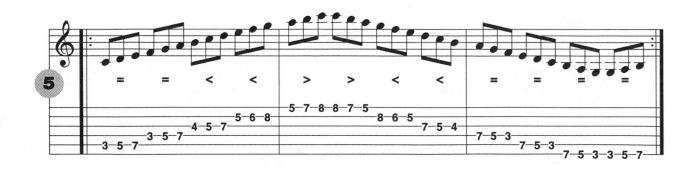

Open strings

You probably noticed that one format (# 3 in C major above) involves **open strings**. This obviously changes **fingering items**, to become :

normal	=	0 2 4	(open string, middle, little finger)
or		0 1 3	(open string, index, third finger);
open	<	0 1 3	(open string, index, third finger);
closed	>	0 1 2	(open string, index, middle finger)
or		0 2 3	(open string, middle, third finger).

Select the most confortable fingering wherever you have the choice. Keep an ascending left hand motion (left to right for the right-handed), in other words, avoid coming back to first position once you've shifted to second position on your way up the strings. This is called **"diagonal playing"**.

Your playing will also benefit from the use of open strings, that produce a specific sound and allow some fingering tricks for fast phrases as used in country, bluegrass, hard-rock, classical and other styles.

Open strings should be practiced for that purpose any time they can be included in the scale formats of various keys.

E major, format 1

D major, format 2

B major, format 4

A major, format 5

G major, format 6

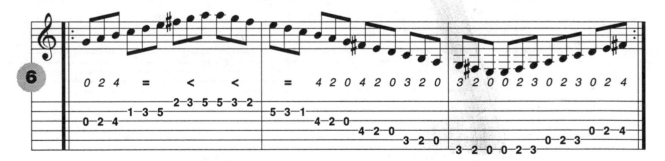

F major, format 7

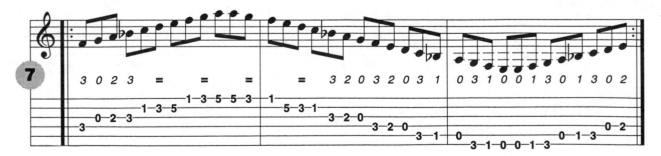

Ascending motion

 Format shifts

Once you've mastered the 7 formats in all 12 keys, you need to practice ways of **connecting** them, keeping in mind diagonal playing, as defined on page 42.

Here are the 7 **ascending format shifts**, in G major:

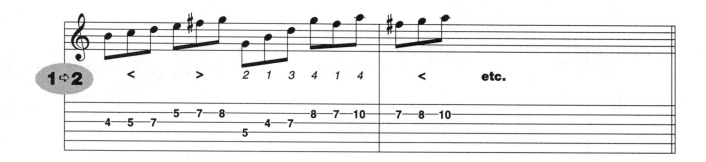

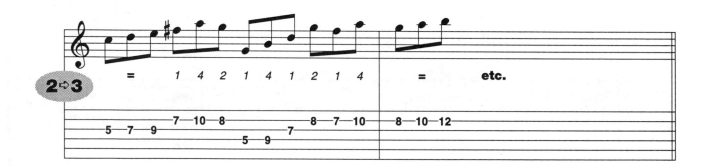

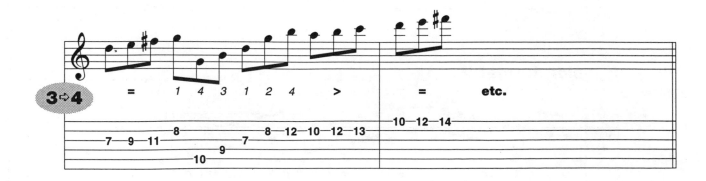

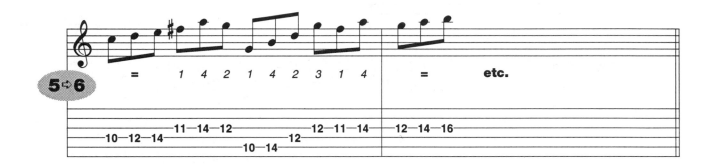

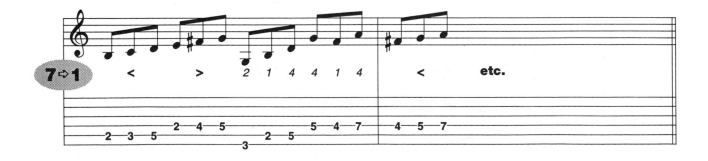

Work out the 7 format shifts above and transpose them in every key before you move on to the complete ascending study.

Study

Here is a "study" - a musical piece designed for specific instrumental practice - simply made out of the seven formats and shifts, in the key of G major. Format numbers appear above the staff for this **ascending exercise** on the whole fingerboard.

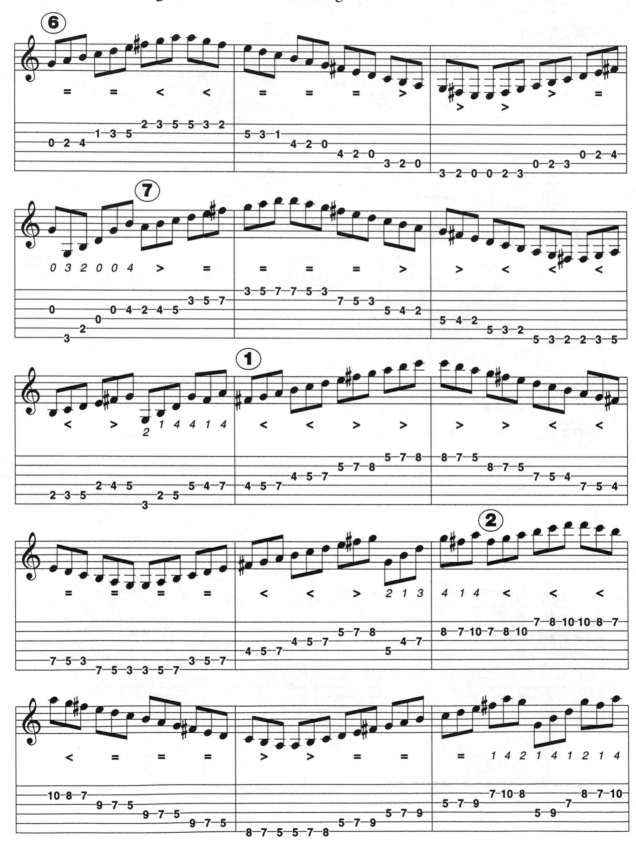

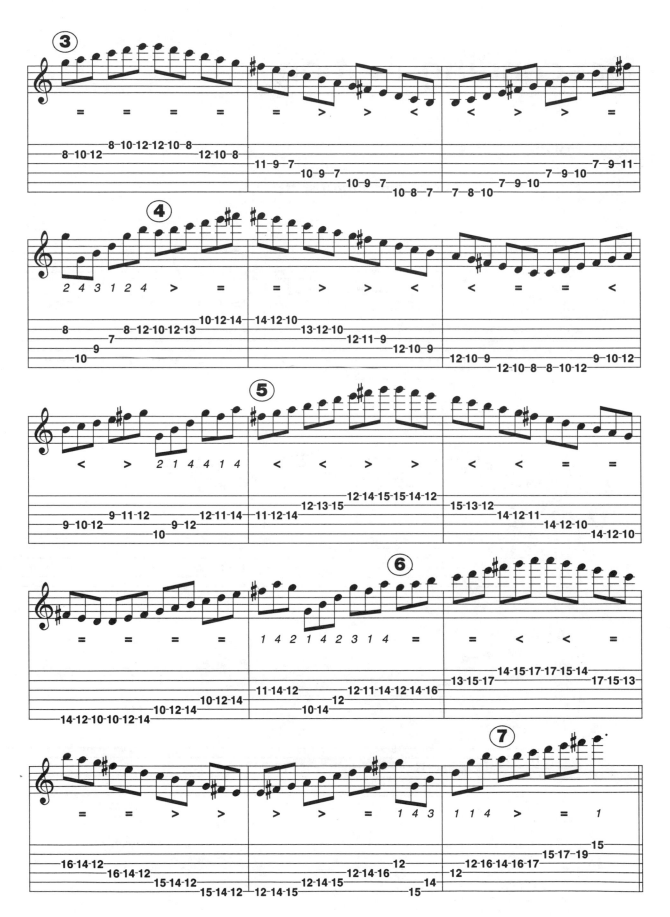

Transpose and practice in all 12 keys.

Descending motion

 Format shifts

Now we have the 7 **descending format shifts**:

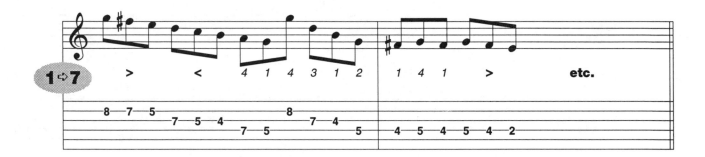

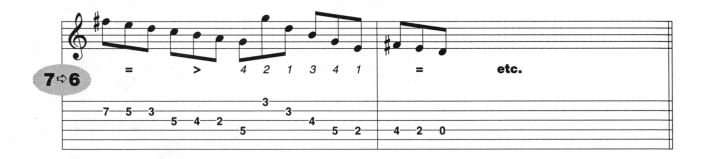

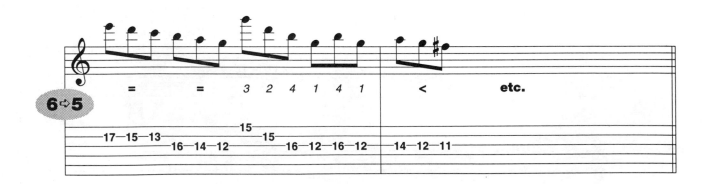

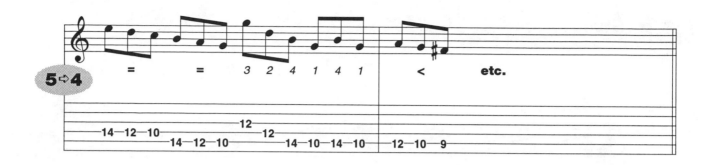

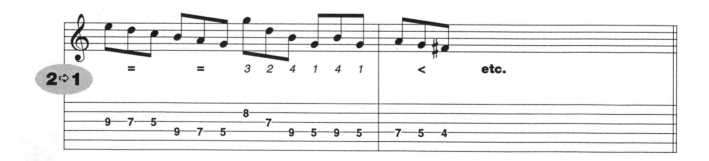

17 Study

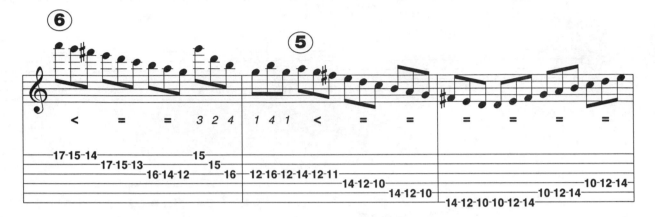

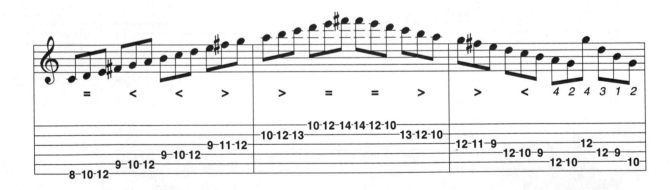

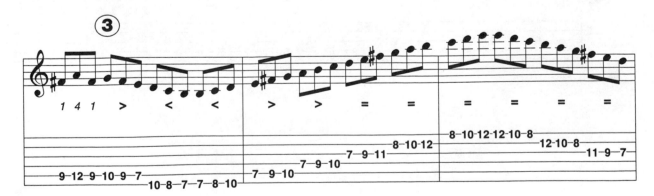

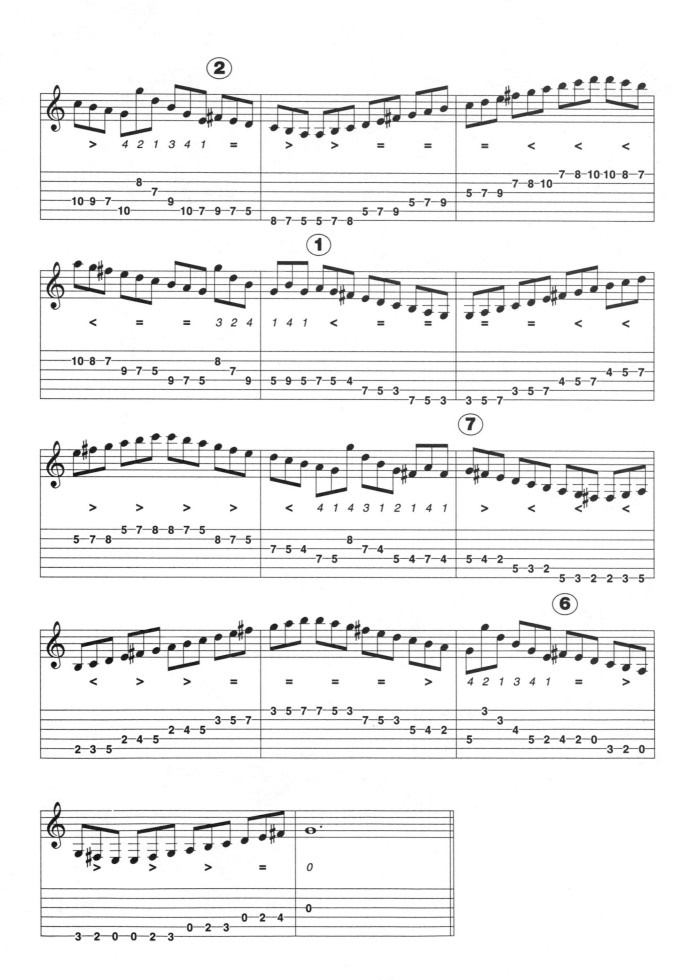

6

Major Scales:
Complete Study
& Application

Technical exercise: groups of 4

This third technical exercise will help strengthen up two vital assets: fingers **power** and **independence**. As you probably noticed, being comfortable using all four fingers is important for a clean sound and a smooth phrasing.

Only the tablature appears below. The notes themselves being unimportant in such gymnastics! The bottom line is: one fret, one finger, with all possible combinations played up and down.

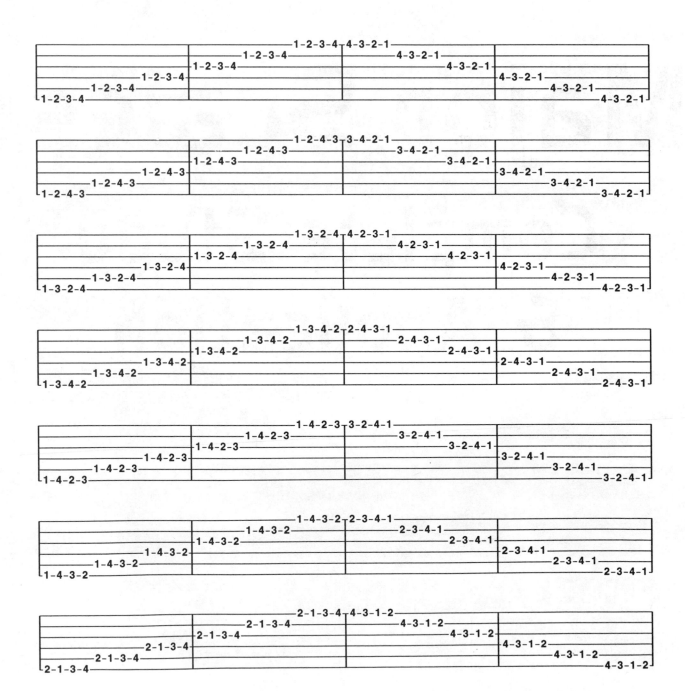

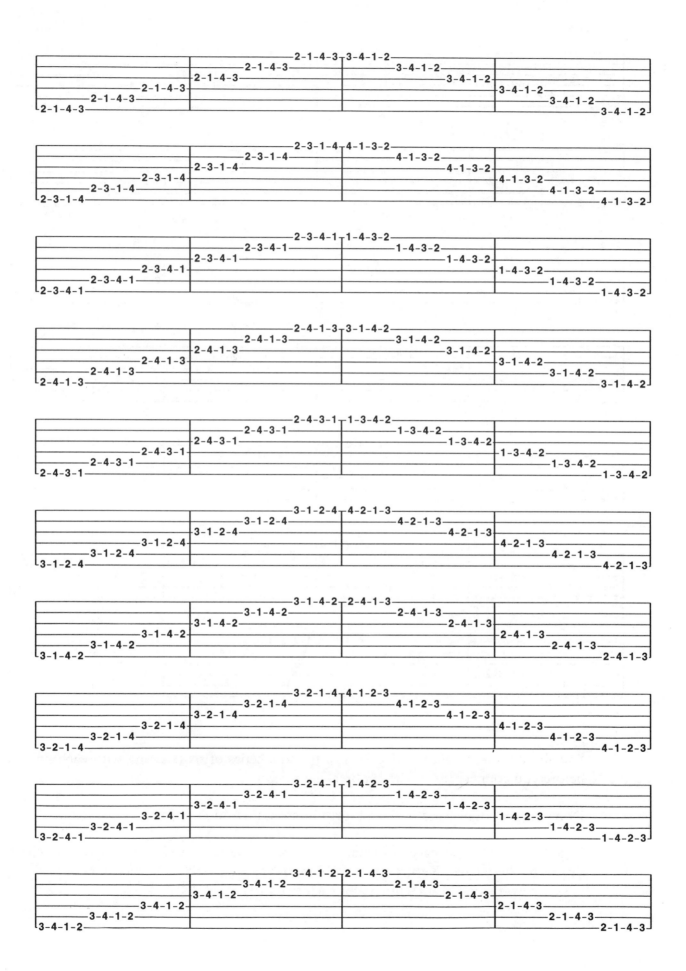

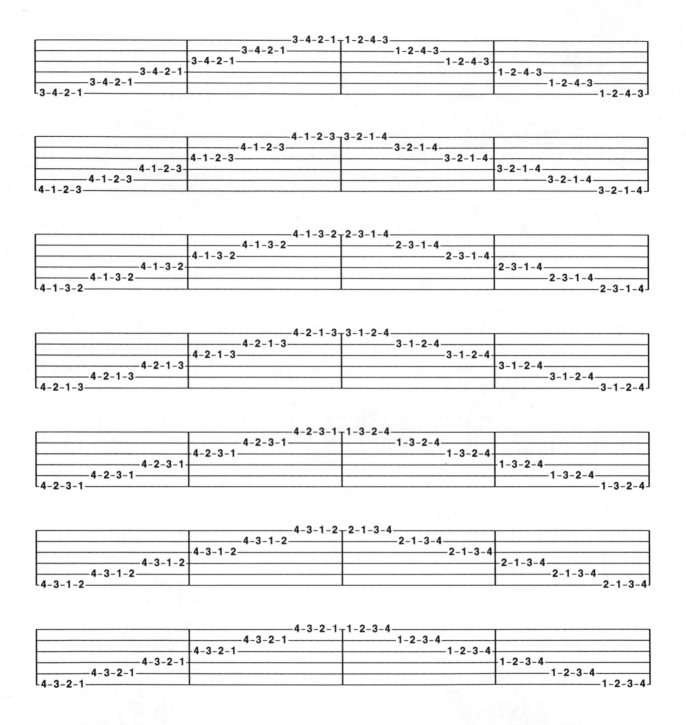

You should, first of all, practice each of the four series of six (starting with each finger) before you connect them without breaking tempo.

Don't forget : right hand back and forth motion, metronome, comfortable tempo...

Page 64 shows a summary of the above 24 combinations, as well as a progression chart similar to the one you've already used. Tempos are suggested for sixteenth note playing, in other words one beat (4 notes) for each string.

Complete study

This exercise combines ascending and descending motions to form a **major scale study** on the **whole fingerboard**.

At this point, you must get used to starting from the middle area of the fingerboard, then playing diagonally up and down, and back up again to the starting note.

The 12 **starting points** are:

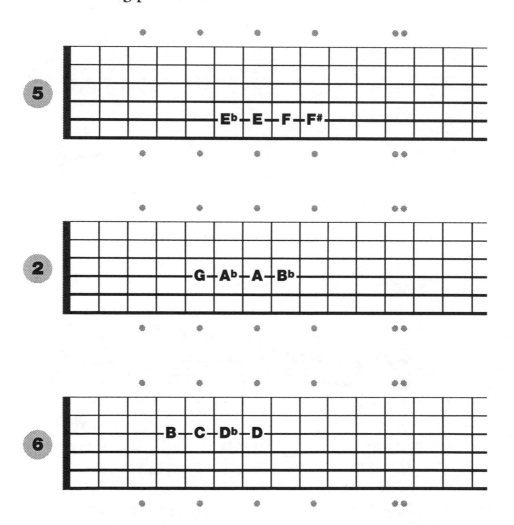

The first format will vary, as you can see, depending on the chosen key, between 5, 2 or 6 as shown on the diagrams above.

The outer edge formats - diagonally up and down, which may include open strings - depend on the key. We will remain on these at least one complete run up and down, whereas intermediate formats may not be played entirely across the six strings according to the format shifts.

The example below is the complete D major scale study.

Format 2 is the furthest (at both ends) while descending format 5 is confined to one octave, which allows us to connect the two shifts - 6 to 5 and 5 to 4 - that are by the way identical an octave apart.

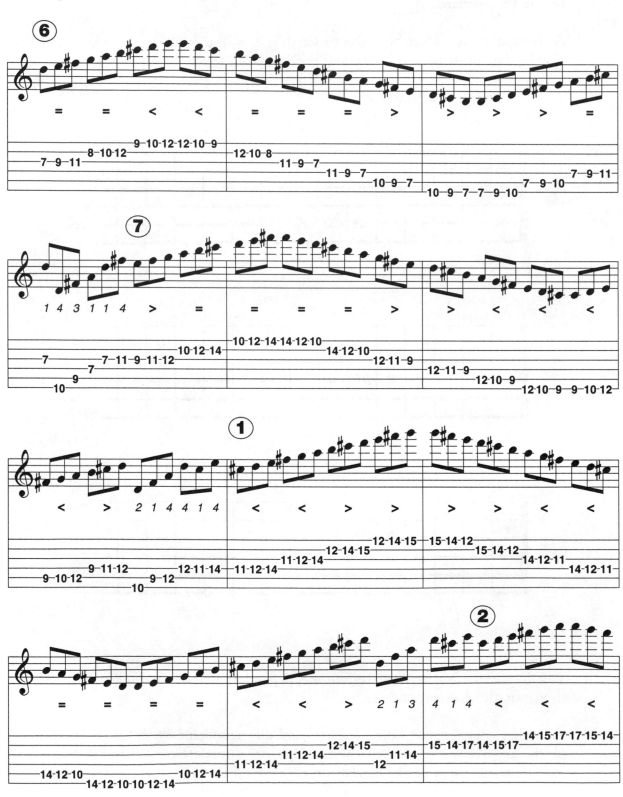

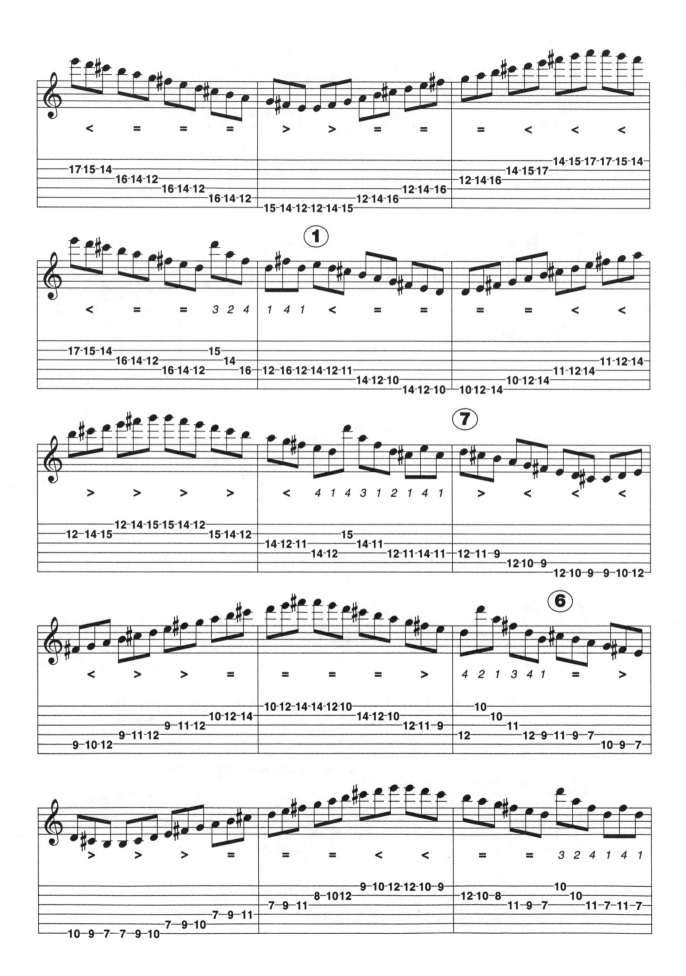

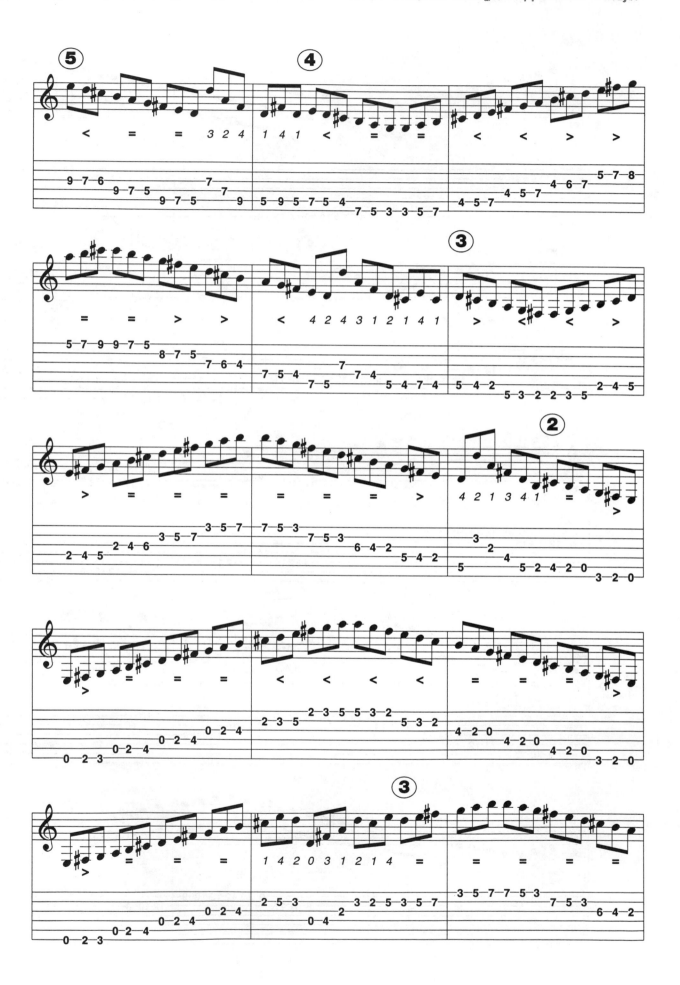

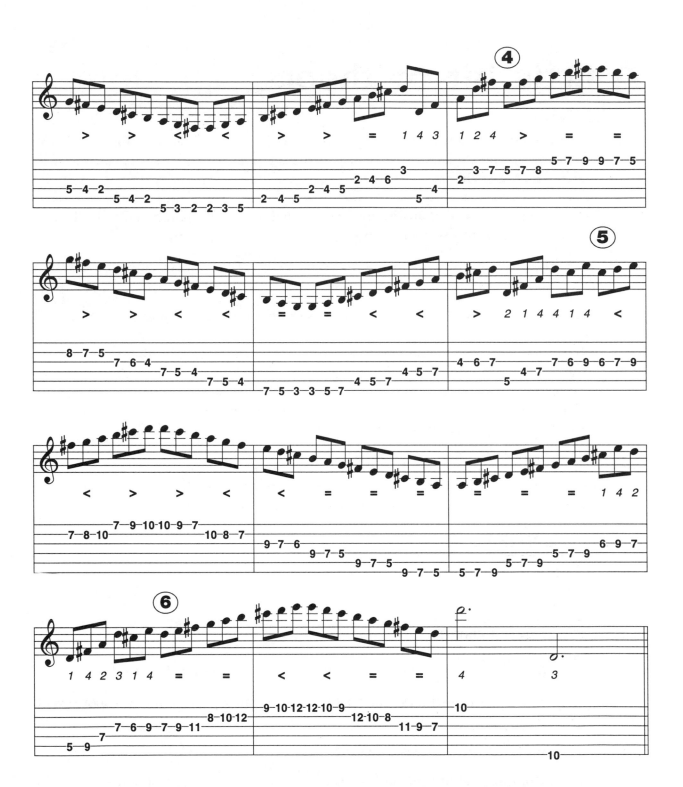

You can design studies for the other keys yourself, combining the 7 formats, the 7 upward format shifts, the 7 downward format shifts and the 12 possible starting points ; always apply the basic rules we've seen so far, including open string use every time you can.

A little bit of theory

There are two main ways to use a scale in a solo. The first is improvisation exercises #1 and #2 style, which you are familiar with. Its purpose is to improvise using the scale that belong to the same **key** as the chords.

The second way is to improvise over each **chord** with "its" appropriate scale. There are pluses and minuses for this second method:

1 - Plus: as a starting rule, you don't need to worry about keys, since you choose your scale from the chord name;

2 - Minus: scales changes occur much faster since every chord means a new scale.

It is actually best to master both approaches and to be comfortable switching from one to the other.

This is the reason why the following improvisation exercises will rely on the second technique which is most popular in jazz improvisation.

To learn how to improvise "by chords", you must know their main types. There are three basic chord sounds and you'll need to train your ear to recognize them. Hearing and understanding their differences is vital for accompaniment as well as for improvisation.

These three types are:

1 - Major chords;

2 - Minor chords;

3 - Dominant chords.

A chord type is defined by the **intervals** each note forms with the chord root.

❀ A **major** chord includes a major third and no minor seventh. The major seventh may be included;

❀ A **minor** chord includes a minor third;

❀ A **dominant** chord includes a major third and a minor seventh. It is called "dominant" because it generally establishes the key in a chord progression.

Improvisation exercise #3

The major scale can be used for **key** improvising, as a substitute for the pentatonic, but its most interesting use is in **chord** improvising, on the corresponding major chord : C major scale over C, D major scale over **D**, etc.

Here comes our third improvisation exercise, which is : **major scales** over **major chords**.

1 - Write down your own progression, composed exclusively of various major chords (4, 8 or 16) without worrying about keys. 4 beats per chord.

2 - Learn it.

3 - Record it (if you're by yourself) or have your fellow guitarist or pianist play it for you.

4 - Find on the fingerboard the seven formats for each needed major scale.

5 - Practice each format with a metronome, playing steady eight note.

6 - Same thing over each chord of the progression.

7 - Improvise over the chord changes, using only the major scales you've practiced.

8 - Improvise freely over the chord changes.

Pre-recorded changes

The two chord progressions for improvisation exercise #3 are :

19 **Chord Progression 1**

| C | A | Eb | G |

20 **Chord Progression 2**

| Db | F | B | E |
| A | D | Gb | Ab |

Technique exercise summary and chart

1 2 3 4	4 3 2 1
1 2 4 3	3 4 2 1
1 3 2 4	4 2 3 1
1 3 4 2	2 4 3 1
1 4 2 3	3 2 4 1
1 4 3 2	2 3 4 1

2 1 3 4	4 3 1 2
2 1 4 3	3 4 1 2
2 3 1 4	4 1 3 2
2 3 4 1	1 4 3 2
2 4 1 3	3 1 4 2
2 4 3 1	1 3 4 2

3 1 2 4	4 2 1 3
3 1 4 2	2 4 1 3
3 2 1 4	4 1 2 3
3 2 4 1	1 4 2 3
3 4 1 2	2 1 4 3
3 4 2 1	1 2 4 3

4 1 2 3	3 2 1 4
4 1 3 2	2 3 1 4
4 2 1 3	3 1 2 4
4 2 3 1	1 3 2 4
4 3 1 2	2 1 3 4
4 3 2 1	1 2 3 4

Date	Tempo	Times through
	52	1

Date	Tempo	Times through
	76	2

7

The Dorian Mode

Modes

For any given scale, its **modes** are all the scales you can build from its name notes, starting from each step of the original scale. Therefore we will get as many modes, including the scale itself, as there are notes in it.

Let's take our good old C major scale, starting from step 2, which is the note D:

D   E   F   G   A   B   C

The **intervals** between these steps are obviously the same since the notes are left untouched, the distance between them and our new tonic D, however, will be different from what they were in C major with the tonic C.

Here are the seven modes we get from the diatonic major scale, and the associated intervals:

1 - ionian (the major scale by itself)

l tone   l tone   ¹/2 tone   l tone   l tone   l tone   ¹/2 tone

2 - dorian

l tone   ¹/2 tone   l tone   l tone   l tone   ¹/2 tone   l tone

3 - phrygian

¹/2 tone   l tone   l tone   l tone   ¹/2 tone   l tone   l tone

4 - lydian

l tone   l tone   l tone   ¹/2 tone   l tone   l tone   ¹/2 tone

5 - mixolydian

l tone   l tone   ¹/2 tone   l tone   l tone   ¹/2 tone   l tone

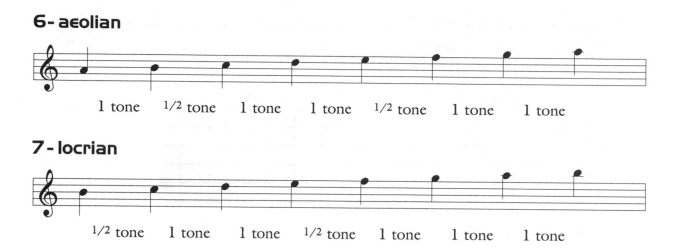

6 - aeolian

1 tone   1/2 tone   1 tone   1 tone   1/2 tone   1 tone   1 tone

7 - locrian

1/2 tone   1 tone   1 tone   1/2 tone   1 tone   1 tone   1 tone

Dorian mode

In the above modes, some are more useful than others. The most popular ones are, aside from the **ionian** a.k.a. major scale, **dorian** and **mixolydian**. These are the two diatonic major scale modes that we will learn and practice in this method.

Needless to say that our seven modes are all seven notes scales - our basics regarding major scale practice will then apply as well. The most important is that the 7 diatonic **formats**, as described in Chapter 4, will be exactly the same for all of them.

Since the notes are the same, the actual shapes will remain, the only difference being format **numbers.**

Let's take as an example **C dorian**, format **5** :

You can see that this scale is exactly the same as **Bb diatonic major**, format **6.**

In other words, here's how to get a **dorian format** (examples are in **C**):

1 - Apply the desired **tonic pattern** to the **tonic** (e.g. **C** format **3**):

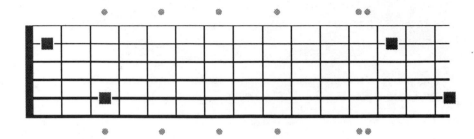

2 - Find out the **major diatonic shape** for the next format (desired + 1, here major format **4**):

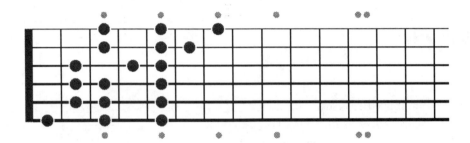

3 - Apply it to the tonic pattern (here we get **C dorian**, format **3**):

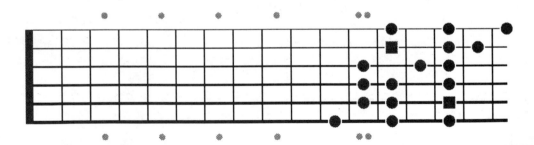

We can see that the dorian mode rule is **major X format over X-1 tonic pattern = dorian format** or, to make a long story short:

major - 1 = dorian

What a relief to think that all your hard work memorizing the seven major scale formats was actually learning dorian formats as well!

So we don't need to go into further details here about them.

Format shifts: harmonic functions

Though the formats are the same with different numbers, the ascending and descending **format shifts** will change. The bottom line is to refer the scale to its **tonic.** Otherwise, what would be the interest of giving a different name to a scale made of the exact same notes ?

This question illustrates the most common misundertanding musicians bump into when it comes to studying modes.

Here's the answer : when you switch tonics, the intervallic structure is modified, giving new applications to the scale. The **dorian** mode, for instance, is clearly a **minor** scale since its third step is a minor third away from the tonic. Big difference with **ionian** which is, as its other name indicates, a **major** scale.

This difference will be emphasized further when we'll use that new scale for improvisation but we can apply it right away to format shifts. Going back to our chapter 5 major **studies**, we can see that each little motif we use to connect formats diagonally is based upon a special construction derived from the major scale, called an **arpeggio** :

An **arpeggio** is itself a "mini" scale exclusively made of notes that make a **chord**. The arpeggio's name is the chord's name. It is actually a sequence of the chord notes played one after the other. In the series *The Guitar Scales,* volume 3 will entirely with arpeggios.

The above example is the **C major** arpeggio, made of the **C** chord notes. This sequence is the basis of the format shifts that were part of our C major scale studies.

This is the scale we used to play over the **C** chord in improvisation exercise #3, both being harmonically linked. Our format shifts thus underlined the major scale's main **harmonic** function.

In a similar way, dorian being **minor**, our new format shifts will use the **minor arpeggio**, e.g. in C:

Dorian format shifts

22 Here are the 7 ascending dorian format shifts, in G minor:

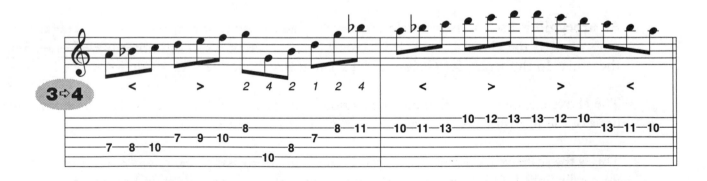

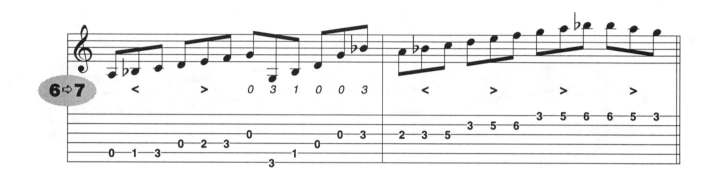

And these are the descending dorian format shifts, still in G minor:

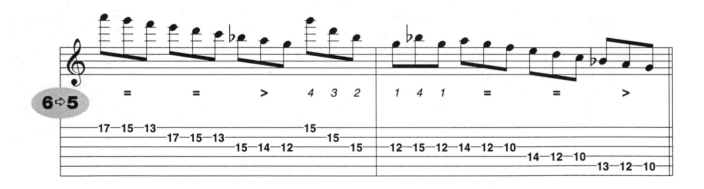

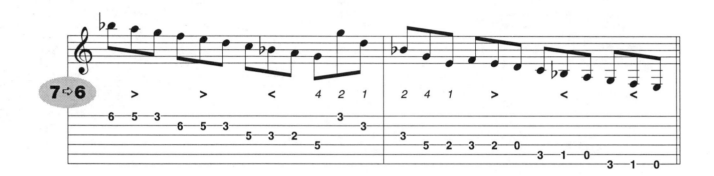

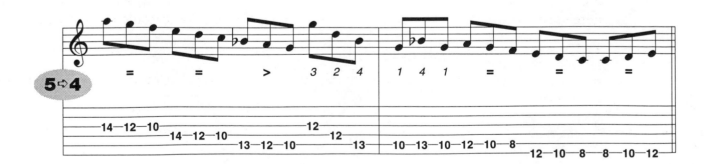

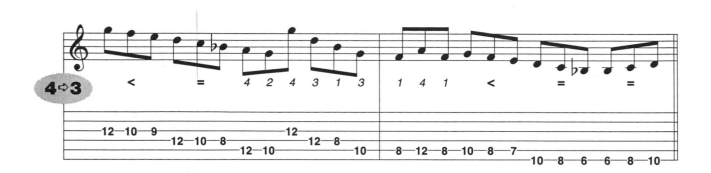

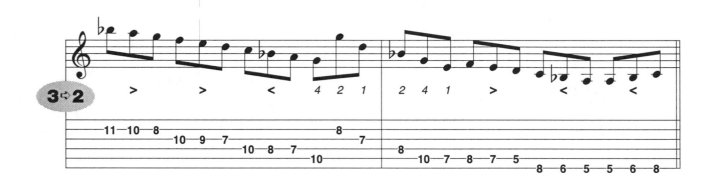

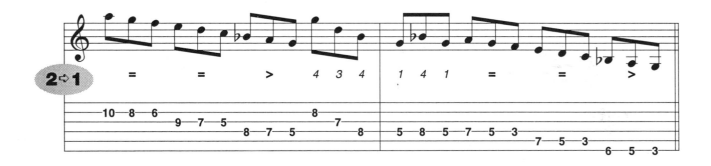

Use these to compose, learn and practice the ascending and descending studies and the **complete study** for all 12 keys, applying the basics we've used for the diatonic major scale:

✿ Use **open strings** every time you can (F# dorian format 7, E dorian format 1, etc.);

✿ One complete diagonal run up, down and back up again for the two **furthest** formats (upper and lower);

✿ Starting point / ending point using the same locations already defined for the major scale (chapter 6).

8

Dominant Scale

Mixolydian mode

Now that we've learned the major scale (ionian mode) for playing over major chords and the dorian mode for minor chords, we might as well expand our musical vocabulary with a **dominant** scale, aimed at 7 type chords.

The **mixolydian** mode - diatonic major mode #5 - seems to fit that purpose perfectly.

Let's take a look at the **intervals** each of its steps makes with the tonic (e.g. G):

The two dominant characteristic intervals are present, as defined in chapter 6: **major third** and **minor seventh** (here, B and F).

The mixolydian mode will then be our "dominant scale", which may be a less scientific but fairly clear wording.

All the previous chapter principles for dorian apply to mixolydian as well, except, once again, for **format numbers**.

For example, dominant format 1, will be derived from the "major" format **5**, whose format 5 lowest note is naturally the scale's 5th step. This same note here becomes our new tonic for mixolydian mode... exactly like, as you probably know, dorian format 1 looks like a major format 2, since dorian is built on the scale's 2nd step.

$5 + 3 = 8$ or rather 1 for our purpose, therefore the rule for turning a major format to a dominant one is **major X format over X + 3 tonic pattern = dominant format,** in other words:

major + 3 = dominant

To illustrate this formula, let's go back to the trick we used before, but this time with **X + 3** mixolydian instead of **X - 1** dorian:

1 - Apply the desired **tonic pattern** to the **tonic** (e.g. **E** format **4**):

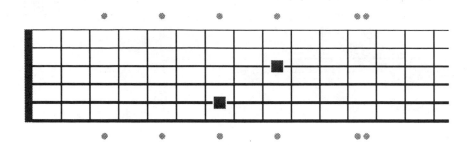

2 - Find out the **major diatonic** format 4 - 3 = 1:

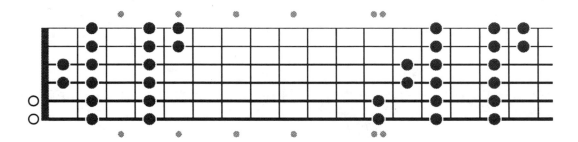

3 - Apply it to the tonic pattern (here we get **E dominant** format **4**):

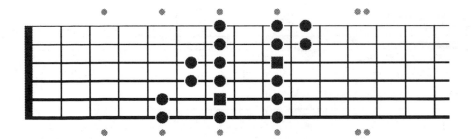

Format shifts

The connection from one format to the next will of course use the dominant **7 arpeggio**. Here is a **C7** arpeggio:

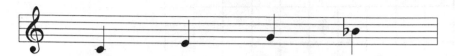

Since we now play four notes to include the necessary minor 7th, we will sometimes need to add a note to keep the logic of beginning the next format with three notes on the same string.

This extra note will be the **ninth** (D in the example) whose sound fits **7** type chords well in most instances.

Here are the ascending dominant format shifts, in C:

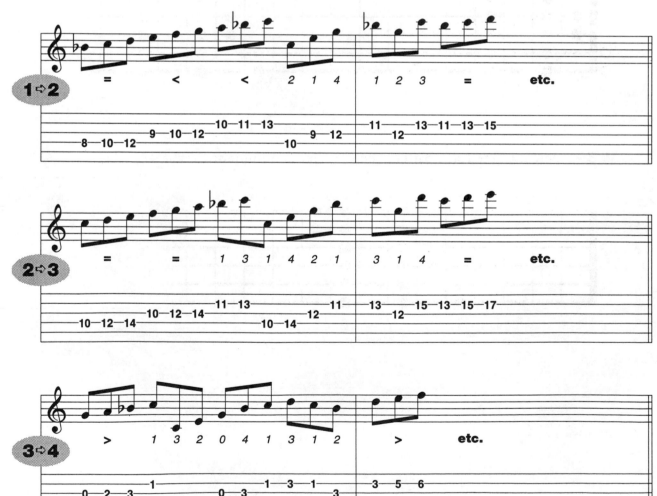

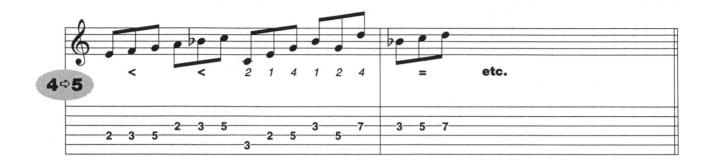

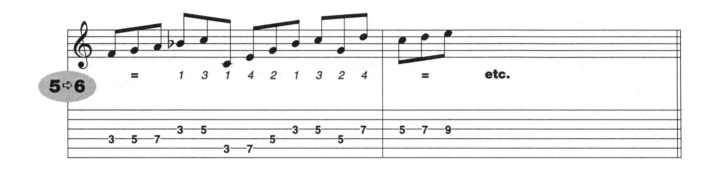

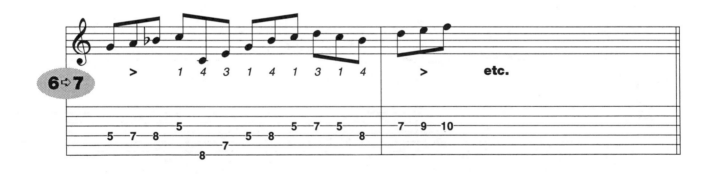

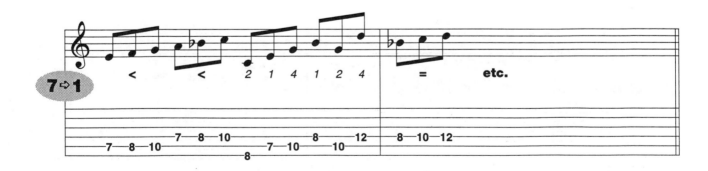

Let's keep in mind that this book uses the following fingering patterns system:

< means 1 2 4;

= means 1 2 4 (with an extra fret between 1 & 2);

> means 1 3 4.

These fingerings will always be the same regardless of the string and position, with the obvious exception of open strings situations.

25 Here are the descending dominant format shifts:

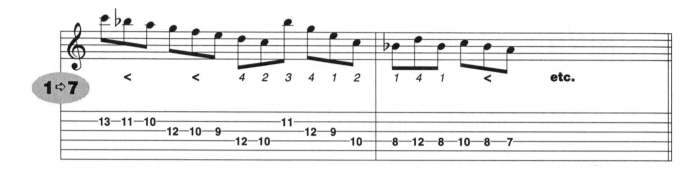

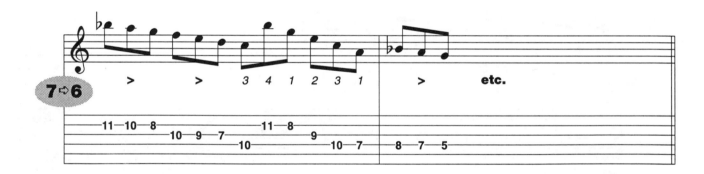

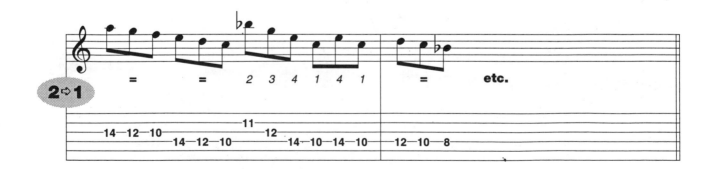

You can notice that in all but 5 to 4 format shifts, the notes are quite similar to our chapter 5 descending major scale, except of course for the 7th (B) that becomes minor (Bb) but also the tonic (C) which is replaced by the minor 7th to initiate the descending arpeggio.

Open strings are included as usual: in C dominant, they will occur on format shifts 3 to 4 and conversely. You will need to adapt your fingerings when transposing to other keys. Let's take a look at A dominant upward shift 3 to 4, which becomes:

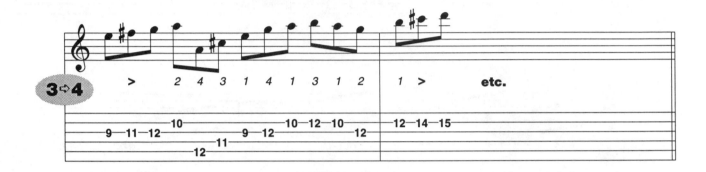

While A dominant downward shift 4 to 3 becomes:

Your turn, for designing studies - ascending, descending and complete - in all 12 keys!

Improvisation exercise #4

The dominant scale is used over dominant (**7**) type chords.

The dorian mode over minor (**mi** or **mi 7**) chords.

As far as the major scale is concerned... well, you already know what to do with it!

Our fourth improvisation exercise will then be: **3 chord types, 3 scales**.

1 - Write down your own progression, composed of various chords (4, 8 or 16) without worrying about keys. Use at least one major or major 7, one minor or minor 7 and one 7.

2 - Learn it (4 beats per chord).

3 - Record it (if you're by yourself) or have your fellow guitarist or pianist play it for you.

4 - Find out on the fingerboard the seven formats for each needed scale (major, dorian or dominant).

5 - Practice each format with a metronome, playing steady eight notes for each chord and switching scales every 4 beats.

6 - Same thing over each chord of the progression.

7 - Improvise over the chord changes, using only the scales you've practiced.

8 - Improvise freely over the chord changes.

Pre-recorded changes

The two chord progressions for improvisation exercise #4 are:

26 **Chord Progression 1**

| G ma 7 | C mi 7 | G mi 7 | F 7 |

27 **Chord Progression 2**

| A♭ 7 | C 7 | B♭ 7 | E mi 7 |

| A mi 7 | F ma 7 | F 7 | B♭ mi 7 |

9

Practice Techniques

Once you've learned your scales in all possible formats and keys, you'll need to increase your control and fluidity. The following techniques will help you achieve this.

Groups of 3

Any scale can be practiced in **groups of notes**, which helps master rythm, various left hand combinations, scale memorizing and, ultimately, a better application to improvising.

The most simple system for pentatonics as well as diatonics (including modes) is to practice it in groups of **three** notes, playing three notes in a row from **every step** of the scale, following its order on the way up and down.

For instance, if a scale is composed of the following notes:

1   2   3   4   5   etc.

groups of 3 will be:

1 2 3   2 3 4   3 4 5   etc.   ascending

5 4 3   4 3 2   3 2 1   etc.   descending

This trick allows, by the way, an interesting practice of the **triplet**, or 3 eight notes series in $\frac{6}{8}$, $\frac{9}{8}$ or $\frac{12}{8}$ meter types which, after all, amount to the same thing, since the basic beat in that kind of rythm is dotted quarter notes.

E pentatonic format **2, groups of 3**. Fingerings will obviously have to be adapted for simplicity as we have done below. On the other hand, the tonic will be the starting and ending note, but never on the low 6th string as usual.

A dominant format **2, groups of 3:**

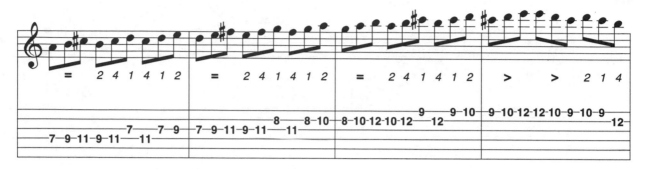

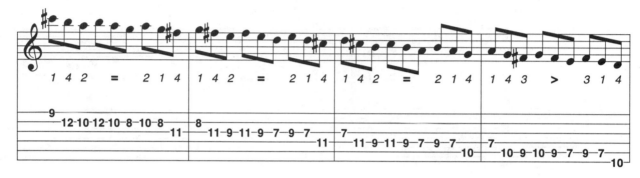

Groups of 4

Same thing with 4 notes in a row from each step. Keeping our example, groups of 4 will be:

1 2 3 4	**2 3 4 5**	**etc.**	ascending
5 4 3 2	**4 3 2 1**	**etc.**	descending

This technique allows an interesting practice of eighth and sixteenth notes.

Bb pentatonic format **5, groups of 4** (eighth notes):

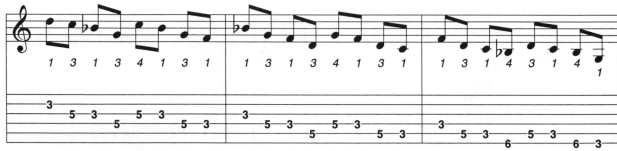

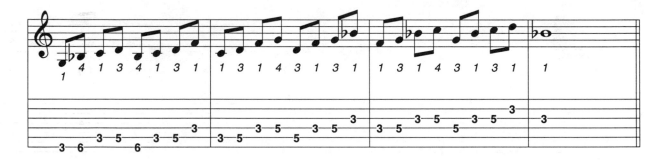

A word about **barres**: in the above example, the G in bar 1 and the following D in bar 2 are both fingered with **1**, which actually comes down to a half-barre, the first finger holding down strings 1 **and** 2.

In such cases you need to plan ahead where your fingers go - which should be a permanent concern anyway - to make sure that your finger is not releasing the first string after having played G, before jumping to the second and play D, which would break melodic continuity...

This barre-based fingering is nevertheless an easy way out, which has its limits: on an electric guitar, holding down the D can make it sound, by a hammer-on effect, at the same time as the G, way before its turn!

A clean and somewhat perfectionist answer is to use two different fingers, one for each note. This implies a healthy and sometimes painful left hand practice.

We actually used this solution for G and C in bar 4, where a 3rd finger barre would have made it much simpler…

Here is the alternate fingering for this exercise, following the "one note, one finger" choice :

1 3 1 4 3 1 4 **2**	1 4 1 4 4 1 4 1	**2** 4 1 3 4 1 3 1
2 4 1 3 4 1 3 1	**2 4** 1 3 4 1 3 1	**2 4** 1 4 3 1 4 1
1 4 1 3 4 1 **4 2**	1 3 1 4 3 1 **4 2**	1 3 1 4 3 1 **4 2** 1

31 **A dorian** format **7, groups of 4** (sixteenth notes) :

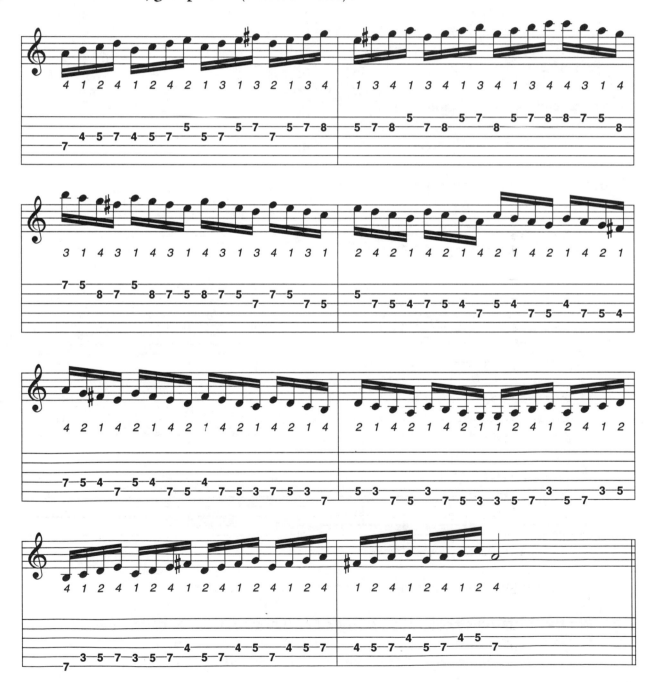

Don't forget **back and forth** right hand motion: one stroke down, one stroke up, or index/ middle finger ou thumb/other finger if you don't use a pick.

Scales can be practiced in groups of any number: 6, 5, 89, 6374, etc. but the most popular combinations are 3 and 4.

Intervallic practice

Another trick is to play each step followed by the note that is X (2, 3, 4...) steps away. Keeping our example 1 2 3 4 5 6 7, the ascending result with a 2 note gap would be:

1 3 2 4 3 5 etc.   descending: **5 3 4 2 3 1 etc.**

Ascending with a 3 notes gap:

1 4 2 5 3 6 4 7 etc.   descending: **7 4 6 3 5 2 4 1 etc.**

32 E♭ **pentatonic** format **3** with a **2 note gap** (following our good old basics):

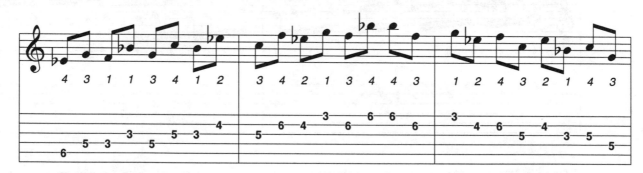

Such assembled notes add up to more or less constant **intervals**.

In the **pentatonic** example, we only deal with major thirds and perfect fourths.

Therefore it will be called "pentatonic scale in **3rds and 4ths**".

With **diatonic** scales, we get **major thirds** and **minor thirds**.

33   **D major** format **5** in **thirds** :

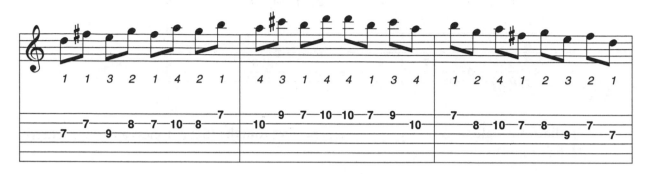

With a **3** notes gap, **pentatonics** will produce **perfect fifths** (7 half tones) and **augmented fifths** (8 half tones).

34   **B minor pentatonic** format **1** in **fifths** :

In **diatonic scales**, a **3** note gap produces **perfect fourths** (5 half tones) and **augmented fourths** (6 half tones).

35 **E dominant** format **5** in **fourths**: